About the Author:

Geoff Thompson has written over twenty published books and is known world wide for his autobiographical books charting nine years working as a nightclub doorman, *Watch My Back*, *Bouncer* and *On The Door*. He holds the rank of 5th Dan black belt in Japanese karate, 1st Dan in Judo and is also qualified to senior instructor level in various other forms of wrestling and martial arts. He has several scripts for stage, screen and T.V. in development with Destiny Films.

He has published several articles for GQ magazine, and has also been featured in FHM, Maxim, Arena, Front and Loaded magazines, and has appeared many times on mainstream T.V.

Geoff is a contributing editor for Men's Fitness magazine, a columnist for Front, and a member of the Royal Court Writers' Group. He is currently choreographing Jim Cartwright's latest play, Hard Fruits, at the Royal Court Theatre, London.

Other books and videos by Geoff Thompson:

Watch My Back – A Bouncer's Story
Bouncer (sequel to *Watch My Back*)
On the Door – *Further Bouncer Adventures.*
The Pavement Arena
– *Adapting Combat Martial Arts to the Street*
Real Self-defence
Real Head, Knees & Elbows
Real Punching
Real Grappling
The Fence
The Art of Fighting Without Fighting
Dead Or Alive – *Self-protection*
3 Second Fighter – The Sniper Option
Weight Training – For the Martial Artist
Animal Day – Pressure Testing the Martial Arts
Tuxedo Warrior:
Tales of a Mancunian Bouncer, by Cliff Twemlow, foreword by Geoff Thompson
Fear – The Friend of Exceptional People: techniques in controlling fear
Blue Blood on the Mat
by Athol Oakley, foreword by Geoff Thompson
Give Him To The Angels
– *The Story Of Harry Greb* by James R Fair
The Art of Fighting Without Fighting
– *Techniques in threat evasion*

The Ground Fighting Series (books):
Vol. One – Pins, the Bedrock
Vol. Two – Escapes
Vol. Three – Chokes and Strangles
Vol. Four – Arm Bars and Joint Locks
Vol. Five – Fighting From Your Back
Vol. Six – Fighting From Neutral Knees

Videos:
Lessons with Geoff Thompson
Animal Day – Pressure Testing the Martial Arts
Animal Day Part Two – The Fights
Three Second Fighter – The Sniper Option
Throws and Take-Downs Vols. 1-6
Real Punching Vols. 1-3
The Fence

The Ground Fighting Series (videos):
Vol. One – Pins, the Bedrock
Vol. Two – Escapes
Vol. Three – Chokes and Strangles
Vol. Four – Arm Bars and Joint Locks
Vol. Five – Fighting From Your Back
Vol. Six – Fighting From Neutral Knees

Advanced Ground Fighting Vols. 1-3
Pavement Arena Part 1
Pavement Arena Part 2 – The Protection Pyramid
Pavement Arena Part 3 – Grappling, The Last Resort
Pavement Arena Part 4 – Fit To Fight

Contents

Foreword

For those amongst us who think kicking in the 'Full Contact Arena', or more realistically, 'The Pavement Arena', is about balletic grace and flashy high kicks, this book is not for them. This book is for the true kicking connoisseur, who wants to learn practical power kicking, which can effectively be applied to street survival, without fears of balance loss, slipping, or having the leg caught in mid-air.

Geoff Thompson, a leading self-protection specialist, has survived countless violent situations, and has had to use street proven skills to defend himself on our increasingly violent streets.

In this concise, professional, and down-to-earth book, Geoff thoroughly explains how to use your kicks in an effective and accurate manner in a street confrontation. Very few people I have met are able to kick as hard and as precisely as Geoff Thompson, who is undoubtedly one of today's most respected Martial Artists.

Anyone interested in the practical aspects of kicking for 'Real Self Defence' will find this book a great asset. Apply the techniques to your training - for your kicking arsenal will not be complete without them.

David Mears
Senior National Coach
(Global TaeKwon-Do Federation)
GIKO World Martial Arts Spectacular Champion

Introduction

Why Kicking?

I would like to start by thanking you, the reader for buying (or if you've borrowed it, thank you for reading) this book. It is said that small libraries make great men, I admire anyone who takes the time to read what a fellow martial artist (or human being for that matter) has got to say. If anyone is offended by my comments on the art of kicking please accept my apologies now before we start - sometimes insults are an inadvertent by-product in books of this genre. My intention is never to offend, only to educate.

Anyone who has read my previous works will know that I'm not a great fan of kicking for the street scenario, and mostly this is where my speciality lies. Some may even say that I am derogatory to the kicker, but that has never been my intention. Honesty, though, sometimes has a way of appearing offensive, especially if it hits close to home. It is my opinion that kicking is the weakest of the main artillery ranges (kicking, punching, grappling), of this I have absolutely no doubt. The pivotal factor with this rather controversial point is not whether kicks are or are not employable, it is whether or not we have the distance to employ them. Nine times out of ten we do not. The majority of confrontational situations happen at a range of about 18 inches, or conversation distance, this being punching range. If mismanaged, punching range quickly degenerates into grappling range and then to ground fighting. A good puncher who understands 'street speak' will enter dialogue, control dialogue and employ a pre-emptive strike that will end the altercation at the same range.

This book is based on nine years of experience working with and controlling violence and violent people. It is also based on over 300 street fights (250 of those were with my ex wife). I have worked the doors with some of the best kickers in the country, probably the world, and we have all reached the same conclusion (some of us learnt the hard way): there is very little room in the REAL world for kicking technique. Then why write a book on kicking? Because a chain is only as strong as its weakest link. If that link is your kicking ability then you are only as strong as that. To be a complete martial artist you must know all ranges, after all you cannot destroy what you cannot create. If you only ever employ kicking technique once in your lifetime in a real fight and it works for you, then it will have been worth it.

Kicking is an effective art if kept in context, i.e. used as part of the support system rather than as an initiating, attacking tool. Kicks are best used in one of four ways:

1) If you are outside of punching range and find that there is a large gap between you and your attacker (there very rarely is) kicks may be used to bridge that gap, even then the understanding should be that the feet are being utilised to set up the hands.

2) Short range kicks can sometimes be used whilst inside vertical grappling range to weaken an opponent before throwing him, or using sweeping kicks from the same range.

3) In the rare circumstance of engagement in a 'square go' on the common, kicking can become effective for taking a boxer or grappler to his or her weaker range.

4) Kicking technique is an unparalleled 'finisher' when employed on a falling or felled opponent.

We are living in a martial arts society that is aroused by celluloid peer pressure, starting way back with the charismatic Mr Bruce Lee who exploded onto our screens with a myriad of spinning, hooking, turning, jumping, even somersaulting kicks that mesmerised, hypnotised and . . . fooled a whole generation of 'would-be's'. This 'movie love affair' has left the subliminal and damaging message that we, as martial artists, not only have to win, we have to do so in style, this of course being synonymous with the superfluous kicking arts. Even the late, great was quick to add that his screen portrayals were fantastical and demonstrated only for 'dramatic effect', a complete parallel to the innovative art he tendered to those wanting workable technique for the 'real' world. What we have to realise as martial artists is that, yes, kicking has its place on the curriculum of 'martial' but it is in the wings as a valuable part of the support system and not on the front line with the main artillery. If I may quote from my book 'Real Self Defence':

"As attacking tools the feet can be both powerful and accessible, though less immediate than the hands and harder to master. Basic low kicks are favourable if you choose to employ the legs as attacking tools. Kicking techniques can be irreplaceably destructive, in theory, in practice 'live' situations lack the space and distancing to employ the 'kick' to its full potential and just by the fact that you are using your legs as attacking tools renders you less mobile."

Great kickers (they are few) will doubtless disagree with me, and as exceptions to the rule probably can and will utilise kicking techniques where I deem them ineffective. If you look at people on a skill scale of one to ten, probably only the nines or tens will be able effectively to employ kicking, the rest, even given perfect circumstances, will not. Even the nine and tens, though, would, I'm sure, agree that when aiming at the masses one is obliged to promote techniques that will work for the majority as opposed to the minority. The distance that you are given in a 'real' situation is nearly always punching range: I can see little reason for changing that range to employ another, especially when the other is weaker.

The foremost problem with the traditionally taught kick is its retraction after connection with target, particularly the contest kick which lingers on contact, long enough to show the referee the scored point. Also, in the dojo the kick is often recovered far too slowly, sometimes the kicker even pivoting on the support leg for several seconds before implanting it back on terra firma. The reason for this laxness? Here no penalty is served up on the lazy kicker. A slowly retracted or thrust kick in a 'live' situation will be heavily penalised by a leg grabbing or forward moving opponent who forces the said kicker over; both former and latter could end in your defeat.

For this reason kicks need to be kept low, hard and retraction sharp, otherwise keep them on the floor where they will be better served as appendages to the hands. To test the viability of your kicks I recommend that you 'pressure test' them. If you worked in a factory making manifolds for cars I could guarantee that not a single manifold would leave the factory without first being pressure tested, as a single fault could affect the workability of the car. We work in a factory called the dojo or gym, we give people technique and character and send them out in to the big wide world . . . without any pressure testing at all. Then we wonder 'what went wrong?' when the said technique and character fail us. The best way to pressure test kicking technique is to allow progressive sparring, that is sparring with no rules. See if you can work your kicks against someone that is determined to grapple you, or box you unconscious, or elbow, knee, bite, but, etc. this is the way to pressure test not only kicking but also character.

Kicking is the weakest of the main artillery, as a support system it is excellent.

It is a near impossibility here not to repeat some of the material from my previous books, because all of them involve some aspects of kicking; indeed at times I may even quote directly from them if I feel it is relevant, so if you have heard some of it before please bear with me.

One thing I would ask is that you not expect overnight mastery of the techniques herein; it can take a lifetime. This book will give you the route but it is you that has to travel it. I could give you a book on Renoir but it wouldn't automatically make you a great impressionist. The legendary Japanese swordsman MIYAMOTO MUSASHI said, "One thousand days of training to forge . . . ten thousand days to polish."

Whilst this book is based on what I would class as 'street workable', there is also a slight overflow, (drawing, feinting etc.) into strategies that are slightly peripheral to its main aim, hopefully this overflow will help you in the dojo with sparring and partner work because to be honest if I stuck to purely effective techniques I wouldn't fill many pages. Treat this book then as an overview and take from it what you feel will work for you. The techniques you may take or leave but the concepts of real world fighting and the place of kicking therein must be observed and remembered if survival is your prime aim.

Chapter Two

Body mechanics

Power in kicking is generated mostly by twisting, thrusting or (and) extending the hip, and pushing from the Hara, (found just below the bell button) which is the body's centre of gravity. Pushing from the stomach, or Hara, helps to utilise the torso weight when kicking and the leg weight when punching. It is also, arguably, the main source of the much talked about, often misunderstood, chi. Other contributing factors are Kime, (body focus), tensing the working muscles on impact (the foot) with the target, travelling, adding the momentum of moving body weight to your attack, and centre line extension, which is extending your own centre line as you kick (mostly with turning kicks). On the latter two points I shall expand in later chapters.

On a basic level we are talking mostly about thrusting the hip behind the chosen kick and then tensing the muscles on impact to add Kime, giving the kick 'body sponsorship'. This is the same whether you are kicking, punching or throwing.

The foot is only the implement that delivers the blow, the bullet if you like. The body or the gun is the power source, the generator or the engine. If you kick without body sponsorship, as so many people seem to, your kicks will be lacklustre. If you kick using body weight transference it is possible to generate so much power that you will hurt your foot when you kick the bag and probably damage your opponent's hand when he holds the focus pad for you, forcing you to 'pull' your kick. Add to this myriad, emotive aggression (or what Mr Bruce Lee called emotional content) and your power increases once again.

Emotive aggression is putting a bit of that old gun powder 'anger' behind the chosen technique. The bloke who cut you up in the car on the way to work this morning, the next door neighbour who is 'cabbaging' you with his late night parties, your ex-wife (or husband) who insists on interfering in your life even though you've been divorced for ten years (they say you have a wife all your married life though you have an ex-wife ALL your life), all these things that build up inside you, that make you angry and give you ulcers can be used as emotive aggression when you kick. In fact, if you partner with me in the dojo you ARE my ex-wife (though a lot better looking, I'm sure). Just transpose those negative feelings into your technique and you will be hitting harder than you ever have before and also, because you are dislodging these feelings from your system your training session also becomes therapeutic.

In theory body weight transference may seem easy, the hip (left or right side, depending upon which side you are kicking with) follows the path of the elected kick, a right leg roundhouse kick sees the right side of the hip (from an orthodox stance) travelling forward and around, along the same route as the kick, a left round house sees the left hip (from the same stance) travelling around and along the same route as the kick. With side kicks you pivot on the support leg allowing the hip to twist, extend and thrust behind the kick, with the front kick the two hips are thrust forward behind the kick and with the back kick both hips are thrust backwards and behind the kick. Generally the hip, or hips, are thrown behind and in the same direction as the chosen kick.

In practice, of course, it is not quite so easy and requires great skill which is only born from much practice and perseverance. Like a finely tuned engine everything must work in conjunction if smooth running is to be attained and maintained: if only one small particle is out of 'sync' with the rest, smooth running will be lost.

If the hip travels through too soon power is lost, too late and power is lost, if the hip is not fully extended (though this would still be classed as a legitimate technique) power is again lost, if it is over extended balance can be impaired, if you over concentrate on any one factor the chances are you may be under concentrating on other aspects. The best way to perfect all of these aspects is 'flight time', logically the more time you put into the practice of anything the better you will get.

If this all sounds a little confusing take heart and don't be discouraged. If it was easy everyone would be good.

Chapter Three

Attacking tools

In this chapter I would like to give a quick run down of the kicks that are available without too much attention to detail, each of the kicks will be detailed in greater depth in their own chapters. Whenever I list a kick that I feel inappropriate for the street I shall say so, and why. In a later chapter I will talk about angular kicks, that is kicks that fall between one kick or another, i.e. a close round house is a cross between a front kick and a round house.

FRONT KICK

Very basic and effective, especially when directed to the lower regions such as the groin, knees and shins. Balance is not greatly impaired (if kept low) and little skill is needed in execution. May be used as a thrusting kick, attacking with the heel by pulling the rest of the foot back, as a snap kick attacking with the ball of the foot by pushing the ankle forward and pulling back the toes, or by attacking with the instep by pushing the toes and ankle forward, it can also be used as a 'stop hit' by attacking the opponent's kicking ankle, as he kicks, with a stomping action using the inside arch of the foot, the ball of the foot can also be used in the 'inside out' motion of the front inward hook kick.

SIDE KICK

Very powerful and accessible though restricted by its high skill factor. May be executed to the front or the side attacking with the heel or side edge of the foot by turning the attacking foot inward and pulling back the toes tightly so that the side of the foot is taught and prominent. It is also possible to kick sideways with the foot and ankle pushed forward, toes pulled back as with the front kick.

ROUND HOUSE KICK

Very powerful and accessible, with a much higher skill factor than the front kick.

The attacking part of the foot can be the in-step, pushing the ankle and toes forward, or the ball of the foot, pulling the ankle and toes back, as with the side kick, using the ball of the foot as opposed to the edge of the foot as the attacking implement. When using the in-step use the bone at the front of the foot to attack.

BACK KICK

Potentially a very powerful kick. Accessible whilst attacking to the rear, a very high skill factor if aimed at a forward facing opponent. The latter entails much skill and is therefore not recommended for the novice kicker. Use the heel of the foot to attack.

Attacking to the front is a potentially hazardous kick because it is necessary to turn your back for a split second on the opponent when turning, the turning action can also cause disorientation. On a slippery or uneven surface execution of this kick could prove fatal.

BACK ROUND HOUSE KICK

A flamboyant kick missiled like a high side kick that is aimed to the side of the head and then whiplashes back into the side of the head, using the heel or the flat of the foot to strike. This kick is best kept where it belongs on the contest arena. It has power potential but is ridiculously dangerous TO THE KICKER for a real situation, only the foolhardy would bother with this kick (scores a damn good point in contest though).

SPINNING BACK ROUND HOUSE

The same kick with a spin (need I say any more). There is no doubt that this kick can generate a lot of power. For a real situation? Not while I've got a brain in my head.

CRESCENT KICKS

These kicks look great in Kata or patterns but in the real world there is little room for them as attacking tools. If you are competent with the kick it can be useful to knock an appendage out of an opponent's hand. The kick sweeps in an inside arc using the inside arch of the foot to attack, or an outside arc using the outside edge of the foot to attack. Highly decorative, highly impractical (sorry).

ANY JUMPING KICK

Taking one foot off the floor in a real situation is bad enough, removing two is ludicrous. Whilst I agree that there is obvious power potential in these kicks and they seem to work well in the ring and dojo, outside I wouldn't even consider their employment.

AXE KICK

In its raw form the axe involves swinging a straight leg, up high and down onto the crown of the opponent's head, the face or the collar bone using the heel of the foot to attack. In this format I feel that the kick is too risky for the street, easy to slip and easy to get the leg caught. However, when employed as a finisher to a felled opponent it is irreplaceable, for quickness lift only the knee as opposed to the whole leg in preparation.

Greater detail on the effective kicks can be found in subsequent chapters.

Chapter Four

Footwork

All of the forecoming movements are executed whilst in a small, 45 degree, left front stance. If you prefer to lead with the right just reverse the instructions.

The footwork with kicking is slightly different to that when punching in that when kicking you have the safety of that distance as a protective shield. For instance, in punching range it is not advisable to let the two feet meet in manoeuvre for fear of being pushed or knocked off balance, at such close range it is probable that this could happen, at kicking range this is still possible though not quite so probable. Double stepping is not recommended in punching though in kicking it is the norm. The complication lies when you amalgamate the hands and feet, for then we have a paradox. In punching I should avoid changing stance, opting for either the southpaw (right leg leading) or the orthodox (left leg leading), whereas in kicking distance you frequently kick off the back leg forcing the said change of stance, when you place the kicking leg down on the floor in front, whilst this is outside the context of this book the point should be noted and a happy medium found (maybe I should write another book on combining distances?).

As far as footwork goes there is not a great deal to write, as with boxing the steps are very fundamental in theory though actual practice can prove to be difficult. I have always found 'basic' as being synonymous with effective in 'real world' fighting' so with that idiom in mind I shall keep it as fundamental as possible.

Footwork tends at times to overlap into other concepts, i.e. centre line extension, punching concepts etc. so forgive me if I go slightly off the tracks.

To a degree a lot of the steps are slightly telegraphed, this can be lessened by hiding the step with a punch or hand strike which may draw the opponent's attention away from the said step. For instance in the half step, described next, a left jab thrown towards the opponent's face would hide the step and give you a free shot with the kick.

HALF STEP

This step is best used with lead leg kicks, front kicks, roundhouses, side kicks, axe kicks, and back round house kicks, though it is only the very basic of the kicks that I would recommend for the real thing. The half step will do two things:

1) cover distance. The size of the step you take depends up on the gap between you and your opponent.

2) Add power. Logically, the faster you make the step the more momentum/power you add to the chosen kick and the greater likelihood of the kick actually getting through, unblocked. Because there is movement with the kick this step would be classed as a 'travel'.

From a left lead stance (right if reversed) move your back right leg sharply forward and toward your left by making a small step (as illus.), as you replace your right foot to ground lift your left leg and kick (any of the prescribed kicks). The bigger you make the initial step the more the distance and the greater the momentum.

Half step . . .

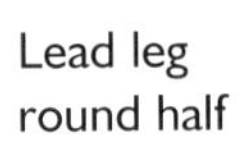

Lead leg
round half

DOUBLE STEP

Oft used by Mr Lee when executing his now legendary side kick, the double step has become one of the most employed steps in today's martial arts. Basically it is just an extended version of the half step, rather than bringing the right leg a half step forward bring it past the lead left leg (as illus.). Some bring the rear leg in front of the lead leg whilst others prefer to bring it to the rear of the lead leg, which is the one I have illustrated here. Personally I like the latter as opposed to the former. As you step through with the rear leg lift the lead leg and kick, ideally with side kick.

SIDE STEP

This step can be used in two ways, using the lead or rear leg to step:

1) To an opponent who is stationary, this then becomes more of a centre line extension than a side step.

2) To an opponent who rushes forward, this then becomes a 'stop hit' (striking the opponent as he is about to hit you).

If you want to kick (usually the kick you use with side step is round house or side kick) with your left leg you should move your right, rear leg across to your own right by making a large (or small) step, as you plant your right foot back on the floor execute the left kick, to kick with your right leg do just the opposite, move your left leg across to your own left by making a large (or small) step, as you replace your left leg back on the ground execute the right kick (as illus.). The size of the step taken can be large or small depending on distancing and the amount of centre line adjustment you want to make and the amount of momentum you would like to acquire. It is important with all of these steps that the flow is smooth, if you stagger between step and kick, momentum is halted and the step worthless. If the opponent is stationary or even moving away from you, you may step forward with your side stepping leg as you step across (to the left or right depending upon which leg you use) to gain more distance. If the opponent is moving forward you may have to step back as you side step out to cover the lost or closing distance.

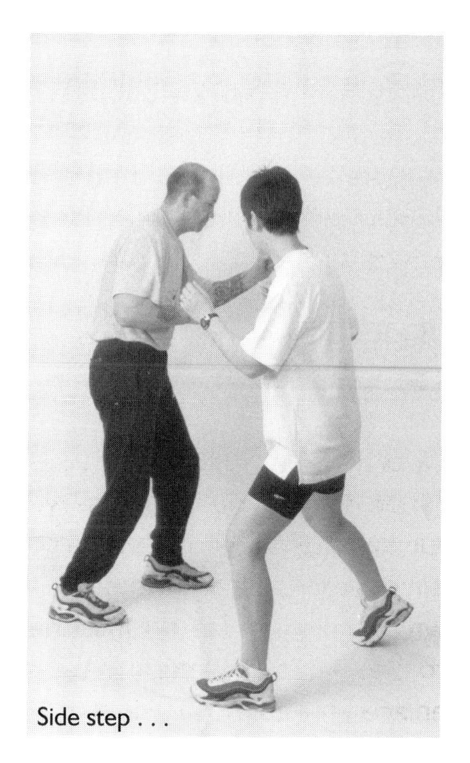
Side step . . .

Roundhouse

Side step . . .

Side kick

BACK STEP

The back step is only used against a forward moving opponent who swallows up kicking range. It is also best accompanied by lead leg kicks, preferably straight kicks, it can also be used as a drawing technique (see later chapter on drawing) to entice a reluctant opponent forward. I prefer the front kick, side kick and roundhouse with this technique. This step adds a lot of power potential to your chosen kick because you have the added momentum of the opponent's forward moving body weight.

As the opponent moves forward quickly step back with your rear, right leg. This will also give the impression that you are retreating, then thrust sharply forward with your attacking lead leg, with your chosen kick.

BACK DOUBLE STEP

The back double step is only used against a forward moving opponent who swallows up kicking range too quickly to employ the back step, it also can be used by a skilled practitioner to draw an opponent. It is best served with straight line kicks, front, side and back kicks, though round house may also work well. Due to the nature of the step it is only viable to kick with the opposite leg to which you step (with the exception of the straight back kick). From the left lead stance move your left leg backwards, sharply until it passes your right foot, quickly place it down on the floor and kick with your right leg as the opponent moves into range. Timing is of the essence with this kick: if your footwork is slow you will be pushed over. Whilst this may not seem to ill a feat in the dojo, outside it would probably prove to be your coup-de-grace.

All of the aforementioned steps, and others that you may like to add can be mingled and bastardised to form others. That's allowed though many might try to tell you that it is not, as my good friend Dave Turton once told me, 'It doesn't matter what colour the cat is as long as it kills mice.' Nothing is cast in stone, if it works for you, use it.

Chapter Five

Areas of attack (targets)

This is one of those subjects that can be argued about all day: where is the opponent/attacker most vulnerable? This can vary according to the person you are facing, though there are usually always safe bets like the eyes, jaw, throat etc., contributing factors like the type of clothes the assailant is wearing, the angle he stands at when you are about to hit him, whether he is behind or in front of you, whether he is standing up and you are contemplating an initiating attack or whether he is on the floor and you are looking for a finisher, etc.

It also depends upon which attacking tool you are using. In this case we are using the feet: the targets that are most vulnerable to the hands are worlds away from those that are vulnerable to the feet. If we were talking about hand range we'd be looking at eyes, jaw, throat etc., none of these is a prime target for the feet unless your opponent is lying on the floor (or perhaps a Pygmy). Sun Tzu tell us that we should "emerge form the void, strike vulnerable points, shun places that are defended, attack in unexpected quarters." But, as I already said, circumstances can and do dictate what is and is not vulnerable. If I'm facing a chap in a crash helmet his head is no longer an option.

Due to the anaesthetic qualities of adrenaline (and probably fifteen pints of Guinness), pain per se is not usually enough to drop an attacker. For this reason attacks should be, in the case of the body, penetrative, striking deeper than surface pain, aiming at the nervous system, or in the case of head, accurate (jaw etc.) so as to cause disorientation or unconsciousness.

Medically speaking, every single part of the anatomy, if severely attacked, could potentially prove fatal. Even if the blow was not a death dealing one, the accidental consequences of it may result in death. For instance a broken nose could send an opponent reeling to the floor where he knocks himself out when his head strikes the pavement (just the initial blow itself could cause a K.O.). If the head does strike the pavement or another solid substance, which from my experience it usually does, a serious concussion or skull fracture may occur, resulting in a possible brain clot or haemorrhage, and perhaps ending in death. Death may also ensue, in this instance, due to the huge amount of blood from the nose clogging the throat during K.O. which in turn stops the flow of oxygen to the brain, again causing death (and believe me there is nothing quite so permanent).

In reality though, breaks, K.O.'s and death are not so common. The human body can be very durable and not an easy vehicle to stop.

I shall list the most common attack areas that I feel are open to the kicker whilst his opponent is in the vertical position; if he is horizontal common sense will prevail. I shall take the text directly from my book Real Self Defence. For more detail on what is and is not vulnerable in real fights try to read my books Watch My Back & Bouncer.

SOLAR PLEXUS

Medically speaking, a severe attack to the solar plexus can cause anything from a deep fissure in the liver to a torn gall bladder or even a complete rupture of the stomach, which may culminate in massive internal bleeding. Due to severe shock or blood loss this can end in death.

More realistically you can expect to knock the wind out of your opponent, at the most. From my experience, body shots, certainly the higher body (unless applied to a felled opponent) are, 99% of the time, not 'stopping' techniques and should only be employed when there is no other target open to you (unless you hit as hard as Peter Consterdine). Adrenaline (and lager) with its pain reducing qualities, builds a brick wall around the body deeming it impervious to all but the most severe of blows. I have also found, to my detriment, that when kicking at the solar plexus it is very easy to get your foot caught. Better to aim lower where the opponent will have trouble grabbing the leg.

JOINTS

All joints are vulnerable to attack, but are largely too well protected by surrounding muscle, accuracy has to be very good to do any real damage. In theory it should be easy to kick a knee joint out of place, in practice you never see it happen. Knees and ankle damage require a skilled, accurate low kicker. Most people are only used to kicking high (even the waist is high) and lack the skill to attack successfully the lower regions. However, if you do train for joint destruction and make that your speciality then you are more likely to succeed. When facing a grappler I like to kick and break the fingers, a grappler without his grip is not such a dangerous fighter.

GROIN

To my mind this is the most vulnerable area open to the kicker (and we are talking about the groin not the testicles). Anywhere around the lower abdomen and pubic bone is very vulnerable. A severe attack to these regions may rupture the urinary bladder causing shock, internal bleeding or thrombosis, even a clot in the femoral vein, which could ultimately lodge in the lungs causing death. Again, though possible, these are unlikely in reality. In the 'real world' this would be my first line of defence if I were using the feet as attacking tools.

TESTICLES

Supposedly the most vulnerable target of the lower region, the one emblazoned on the front of so many self defence posters and books, 'kick him between the legs, that'll work', well, sadly it usually doesn't. In my time I have kicked, punched and grabbed this supposedly vulnerable area in a bid to 'stop' an attacker, usually to no avail. My lack of success has been largely due to them being so well protected. Attempted infiltrations with foot and fist have been lost either to the assailant's large front leg muscles that sentry the testicles or the assailant's instinctive 'thrust back' action (as a male you learn to do this at a very, very early age). Even in the case of the 'grab and squeeze' (pretty difficult to do with your feet, though) the assailant's underpants and trousers demand an iron grip to get even a whimper (this might not be relevant if you are a naturist). Paradoxically, if you manage to score a direct hit that is an entirely different matter.

The foregoing may lead you to feel that there are not too many vulnerable areas open to the kicker, so what's the point? Personally I don't try and 'stop' an opponent with my feet (though a stoppage would of course be nice) rather I use the feet to set up finishing techniques with the hands (see Real Punching). This is where the feet come into their own.

The most important thing is never to expend energy on non vulnerable areas that are heavily protected by bone or muscle. You may only have one good shot, don't waste it.

Chapter Six

Front kicks

NOTE: Before I go on to talk about and dissect the myriad of kicks on the curriculum I would like to point out that whilst in the dojo or gym arm movement may be an important facet, it is important to try and maintain some kind of guard. In the street this doesn't really come into it because the altercation never usually lasts long enough to warrant employment of guard, unless the fight goes some distance or it is an arranged fight on the common, which it very rarely does or is. To employ a guard before you attack will only serve to warn your opponent of your intentions, losing you that vital edge of surprise.

All the kicks here are described in solo. When using them for real they are best followed or combined with other techniques, i.e. a lead leg round house could be followed by a right cross punch, or even by another kick or a sweep, depending on the circumstances. When kicking off the rear leg you may, after connection with target, place the foot back behind in its original starting position or in front where you may wish to add a combination technique.

BREATHING

It is good to exhale when you kick (the same with any attack). This will add Kime to your strike, feed the working muscles with Oxygen and also regulate your breathing. Because Kime uses muscle tension on the elbow's impact with target it will also prepare you for blows received during execution of your strike.

In description I shall talk about which part of the foot one uses to attack. In a real situation you will very likely be wearing footwear: this doesn't matter, you still make the same form with the foot, the shoes will only help to give your kick more impact and protect the toes from damage. It is advisable to try and practice as often as you can in the type of clothes that you would normally wear - what feels easy in a Gi (training suit) may well be a physical impossibility in tight jeans, or a skirt.

The front kick varies from style to style. Whilst some insist on the instep being used to strike others prefer to use ball of the foot to strike, some systems even endorse the use of the toes, personally I find the latter more than a little painful and prefer to use something that is stronger than the target that I am hitting. In reality no one system has the ultimate front kick (or ultimate system for that matter), different circumstances call for a different kick. Using the instep would be pretty ineffective if I want to attack straight into the stomach though it would be perfect if I was to kick the opponent between the legs, the same the other way around.

I will list the front kicks as I see them and where I feel they are best utilised.

KIN GERI (Front snap kick)
Kin geri is a very basic and very effective 'real world' kick that holds a low skill factor, best used when kicking in a upward, snapping motion, i.e. between the opponent's legs or into a bending opponent's face. Push the ankle forward and use the bone at the front of the foot to strike. For best power potential thrust the hips forward and upward on impact with target. As with most kicks lift the knee prior to executing the kick and retract immediately after connection, if you get your leg grabbed you've got problems in this arena. The shin may also be used to attack as well as the instep.

This kick can be well employed whilst inside vertical grappling range, using the grip you have on the opponent as a power appendage, pulling him into your strike.

MAE GERI (Front lunge kick)

With the lunge kick the ball of the foot is used to strike by pushing the ankle forward and pulling the toes back, lift the knee first and then thrust the hips sharply behind the kick. The lunge kick should be like punching with the foot. Due to the 'lunge' at the end of the kick there is a possibility of getting the leg caught, especially if you kick too high, so sharp retraction after connection is very important. The sooner you can get your kicking foot back on the ground the better. Most kickers lose in real situations because they get caught on one leg, the next thing they know they are eating pavement (not a pleasant taste) so beware, it isn't enough simply to retract the foot quickly: you have to get it back on firm ground. Many kickers are in the habit of pivoting on the support leg for a second or three, but most real fights are over in that space of time.

FRONT STOMP

The stomp can be used to attack or defend, attacking the opponent's shins or knees to strike or attacking the same as a defence when the opponent tries to employ a kick of his own. By pulling back the ankle and the toes and then turning the foot to your right (left if attacking with the left foot) you are able to use the arch of the foot to attack. When attacking lift the knee of the attacking leg, being sure to pull back, turn the ankle and toes, and thrust into the opponent's stationary or kicking leg, again thrust both hips forward at the end of the kick for added power. With the latter defensive stomp to the advancing or kicking opponent, timing is of the essence. This will only come with much practice.

FRONT INWARD HOOK

This is what I would term a rainy day kick, something that may come in handy one day, though I wouldn't count on it. The skill factor is very high and to be honest there are very many other more effective kicks you could use with a much lower skill factor that would be far more suitable, unless you are intending to kick someone who is standing around a corner I would leave this one in the dojo. The ball of the foot is again employed, pushed out as opposed to forward, in an 'inside out' motion almost like an inverted roundhouse kick, said to be good in close; personally I can't see it.

FRONT HEEL KICK

Much favoured by the Chinese systems (don't know about the kick but I love the food) and almost a facsimile for the front lunge kick, employing the heel of the foot rather than the ball. When kicking low I have found this kick to be effective, though I still prefer the ball, when kicking high though it can often cause over-committal which may mean getting your leg caught again. Lift the knee of the kicking leg and thrust forward, pushing both hips behind the kick for added power.

Heel kick

FRONT SHIN KICK

A very basic, economical kick used to attack the opponent's shins as a weakener from close kicking range or inside vertical grappling. Very little knee lift is employed. From kicking range thrust your attacking leg forward, being sure to prepare the foot by pushing your ankle forward and pulling your toes back, on impact with target thrust the hips forward and behind the kick. From inside vertical grappling range simply kick the opponent's ankles with the ball of the foot, the pain reaction should lead you in to a more substantial movement (see Real Grappling).

Chapter Seven

Round house

The round house kick has a much higher skill factor than the front kick, though to the practised kicker it can be a very versatile and damaging tool. The attacking part of the foot can be the instep, the ball or the shin: again there is great argument over which is favourite, they are all as good as each other, and as long as the foot is locked into its position, whatever that position may be on impact with target, it will do the damage. Dyed in the wool traditionalists will tell you that the foot has to be 'this way' or 'that' and if it isn't then it's not right.

There was a huge argument for a long time over a European fighter kicking round house with the instep instead of the ball. Sacrilege!!! Until it was realised that it worked, then everyone was kicking round house with the instep. Rocky Marciano was told off for punching with his famous overhand right hook. No one had seen the punch before, his trainers told him to stop using it,

"But I'm knocking everyone out with it," Mr Marciano protested.

"Oh, all right then, use it," they conceded. The next thing you know everyone in the world of pugilism and even further afield was throwing overhand rights. The Thai's have got it right, they don't care what part of the leg connects as long as it hurts the opponent and doesn't hurt them.

Any target below the chest is a safe and legitimate one. More specifically the ribs, kidneys, lower abdomen, groin, pubic bone, testicles, thighs, knees and shins. The higher the target area, the greater the danger of impaired balance and slow recovery, unless highly skilled.

If you employ the ball of the foot pull back the ankle and toes so that on impact with target the heel of the foot is higher than the toes. If employing the instep push the ankle and toes forward and strike with the bone at the front of the foot, if you are attacking with the shin, position the foot in the same way as when striking with the ball (this will flex the muscle at the front of the shin, protecting it) and alter your distancing so that the shin hits target and not the ball. It is important to lift the knee of the attacking leg high and to your own, right side, (left if kicking left) throw the designated leg in a turning motion and into target by pivoting on the support leg and thrust the hips and hara behind the technique and on impact with the target. After contact quickly retract the leg by reverse pivoting on the support leg, pulling the hips back to the start position and replacing the kicking foot sharply back to the floor.

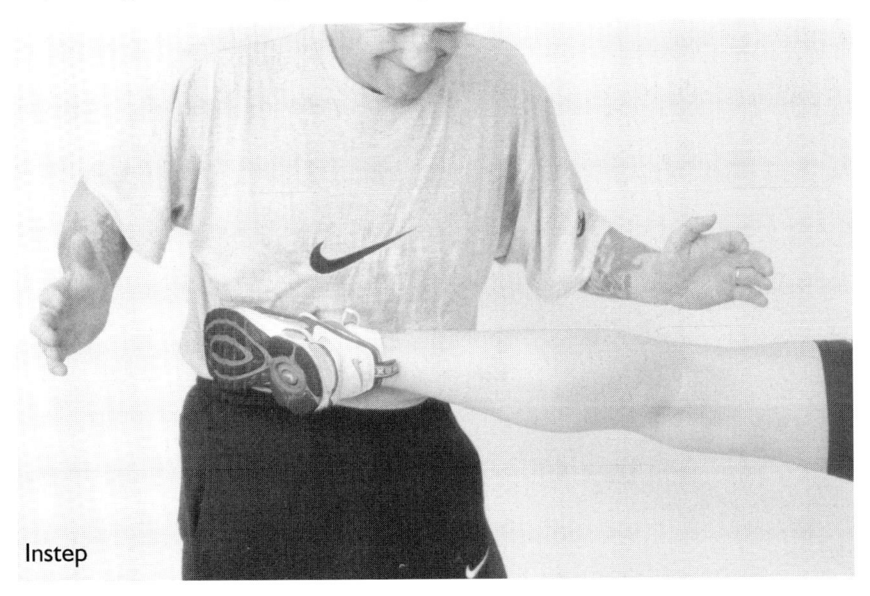

Instep

ball of foot

I am often asked my opinion of the shin round house, personally I find it very effective for setting up bigger techniques like the hands; outside I tend to use it as part of my support system. I have also dropped many people in the controlled arena with the same.

This is largely where the problem lies, people test a given technique in the controlled arena, and if it works there they automatically think it will work outside. This is not normally the case, the only way to be sure is to pressure test it in all out, full contact progressive fighting (where kicking distance is lost quicker than virginity in a Swedish whore house) rather than risk trying it when a real situation hits you in the face like a tornado. Ask someone who has been there what he or she thinks and take heed of the answer. Shin round houses also have a tendency to bring you in a little too close to the attacker than is normally desired, often close enough for them to reach out and grab/punch you. If you are in kicking distance that's the time to kick, if you are going to get close enough to shin kick you are changing ranges, if you are going to change ranges you may as well make it worth your while and go for the K.O. with a good hand strike.

If you are well practised with the round house it can be a brilliant opener or weakener. The better Thai boxers use the lead leg round house like a boxer uses his jab. It can be excellent for making openings or slowly corroding the opponent's will, though this is more of a sparring concept than anything else.

Chapter Eight

Side kicks

This is probably one of the most over rated of the basic kicks and falls well short of effective in an arena that chews up superfluousness and spits it out bloodied and battered onto the unforgivingly cold pavement of defeat. It would take a top level kicker to make this anything other than 'pushy', if I invest in a technique in a live situation I want to see some return on my investment. I don't want to 'push' someone over only to have them to get back up and have another go. I don't want to 'make their eyes water' with something 'flicky' that might have come out of a lucky bag - if I want to make their eyes water I'll show them a peeled union. (COME ON!!! WHO WANTS IT FIRST? IT'S A SPANISH ONE!?) If you're doing it for real you want to be hitting the opponent with the very best, hardest, fastest most destructive technique available to you, you want to hit him so hard that he goes back in time and when he wakes up his clothes are out of fashion.

Having said that if you are prepared to work the technique to destruction and practice very low level kicking this kick could become an integral part of the support system. I know what you're thinking: 'I work this technique all the time in the dojo, I've dropped loads of people with it.' I know, so have I, but the dojo isn't the street it's the dojo. A real situation can explode so quickly and so ferociously that you have little time to think, let alone do anything else. Distances are lost so quickly that suddenly you find yourself 'on your arse' and wondering where 'they' disappeared to.

However, the side kick can be powerful and accessible, though largely restricted by its high skill factor (anything, no matter what, with a high skill factor has little chance of working 'out there'). May be executed to the front or the side using the heel or edge of the foot to strike, by turning the attacking foot inward and pulling the toes back tightly so that the side of the foot and heel is tight and prominent.

When attacking to the side lift the knee of the attacking foot upwards, being sure that you have made the foot ready, and thrust it sideways at the target whilst simultaneously pivoting on the support leg so that the support foot is pointing in the opposite direction to the target, this will ensure full hip commitment. After connection with the target quickly retract the foot back along the same route and replace on the floor as soon as possible, don't pivot on one leg or you'll find yourself on your arse (that's the part at the top of the kicking leg).

If using the side kick to a front facing opponent lift your attacking knee to the front, facing the opponent and thrust it forward, pivoting on the support leg and extending the hip to ensure full hip commitment. Use the side of the foot or heel to strike. Retract the kick quickly and place back on the floor.

When in vertical grappling the side kick may be used to attack a second opponent whilst grappling with the first by kicking out as he approaches. You may use number one opponent as leverage.

Whilst I recognise that the side kick is traditionally taught using the heel or foot edge to strike it is also viable to side kick using the ball of the foot, as you would with front lunge kick. This method gives the kicker extra reach and because it is more pointed than the edge and heel, greater penetration and thus more power potential.

Chapter Nine

Back kicks

Again, the back kick (straight back kick) very rarely comes into play in real world fighting, not because it's not powerful, it is devastatingly powerful, not because it's not fast, it can be very fast, rather it is because a situation is 'in your face', it is so close you can smell it, you have maybe 18-20 inches to play with, there just isn't the room.

To the skilled practitioner the back kick is very powerful and can be destructive, more accessible when attacking an opponent to the rear, though demands a very high skill factor if aimed at a forward facing opponent. The latter requires much skill and is not recommended for the novice. The heel is the attacking tool and serves best when aimed low at the ribs, groin, pubic bone, testicles etc. Many hours of practice are needed to perfect this kick.

When you use the back kick to attack an opponent to your front this can be a hazardous kick because it is necessary to turn your back on the opponent for a split second. From a left lead stance lift your right leg up and bring towards your left, wrapping the instep of the right foot tightly around your left calf muscle. Pivot around on your left support leg so that your back is directly facing your opponent, simultaneously turning your head so that you do not lose sight of him. Thrust the heel of the right foot, propelled by the forward (or backward depending on how you look at it) thrust of both hips, into the target. After connection with target, twist your body around and place that attacking foot quickly back to the floor so that you are now facing the opponent.

If you are using the kick to attack to the rear it becomes safer and easier to employ, though the timing with front and rear can be very difficult. Turn your head around so that you can see the target/opponent (this helps a lot), lift the knee of the attacking leg to waist height and in front of you. Thrust the attacking heel directly behind you and in to the target/opponent, propelled by the backward thrust of both hips following the route of the kick. From this position you may either turn after connection and face the opponent or pull the attacking leg back along the same route to front knee lift and then place the attacking foot back to ground.

I've never really found the room to use this type of kick in real situations though it has been one of my favourites in sparring. I still allow it practise time, if I only ever use it once in my lifetime then it will have been worth it.

As with the side kick the back kick can be useful to attack a second opponent whilst vertically grappling with the first, again using the first as leverage while you kick the second.

Chapter Ten

Stamping kicks

This kick is, as its name implies, a stamping kick, taught in the First and Second World Wars as a means of finishing off a felled opponent, used either with a single or double stamp. I have used it frequently in 'live' situations, sometimes to the head, sometimes to the body (depending up on the seriousness of the situation), always with effect. It is a very dangerous technique that needs much thought before use, as General Sun Tzu said (he nicked all of my material by the way) 'before you wage war, you must first count the cost'. Before you consider the use of the stamp or the axe consider the fact that it is a potentially lethal technique and if you kill an opponent your life is as finished as his (read *Bouncer* for an insight on how this can effect your life); certainly if used full and to the head of a horizontal opponent, in law it would, no doubt, be classed as barbaric and beyond the realms of 'reasonable force'. In most self defence situations I recommend that you hit and run, that sorts the situation out and keeps you sweet with the law, though this is not always possible.

Fundamental, accessible and very destructive, used primarily as a finishing tool but may also be used in vertical grappling to stamp on the opponent's ankle or foot. Lift the knee of the attacking leg high and directly in front of you, stamp the heel of the attacking leg into and through the target.

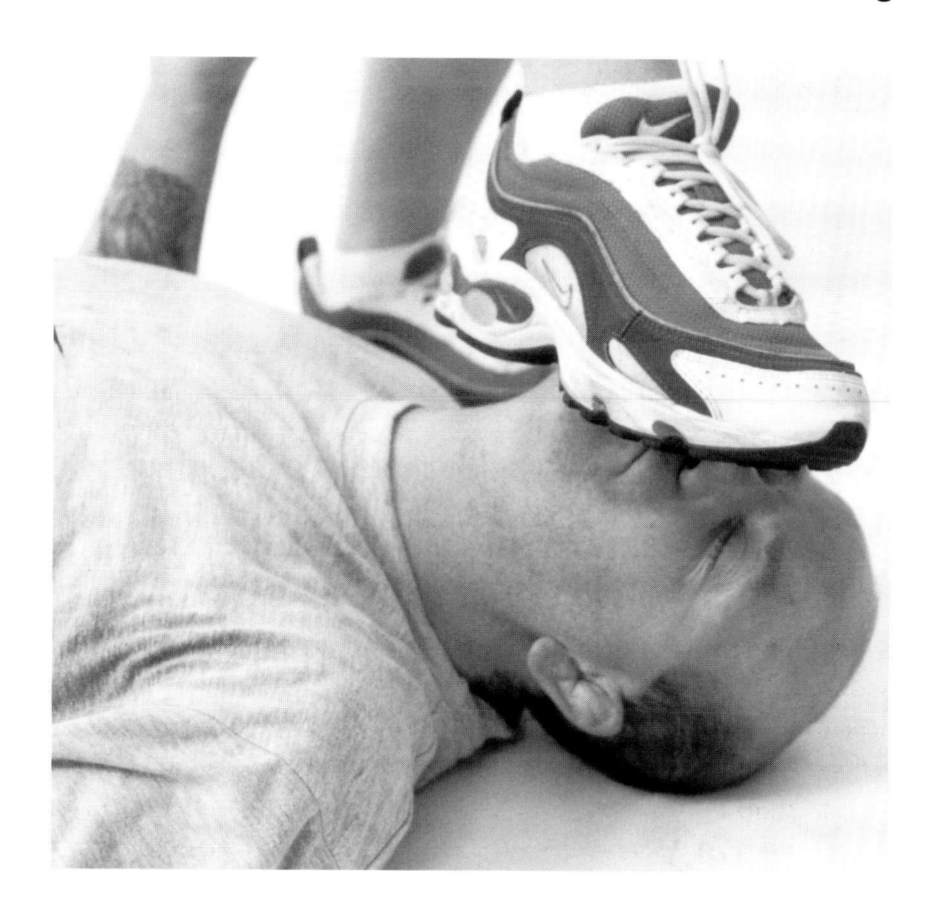

When employing Osot gari (outer reaping throw) to a strong opponent you can use the stamp against the back of his leg to force him over.

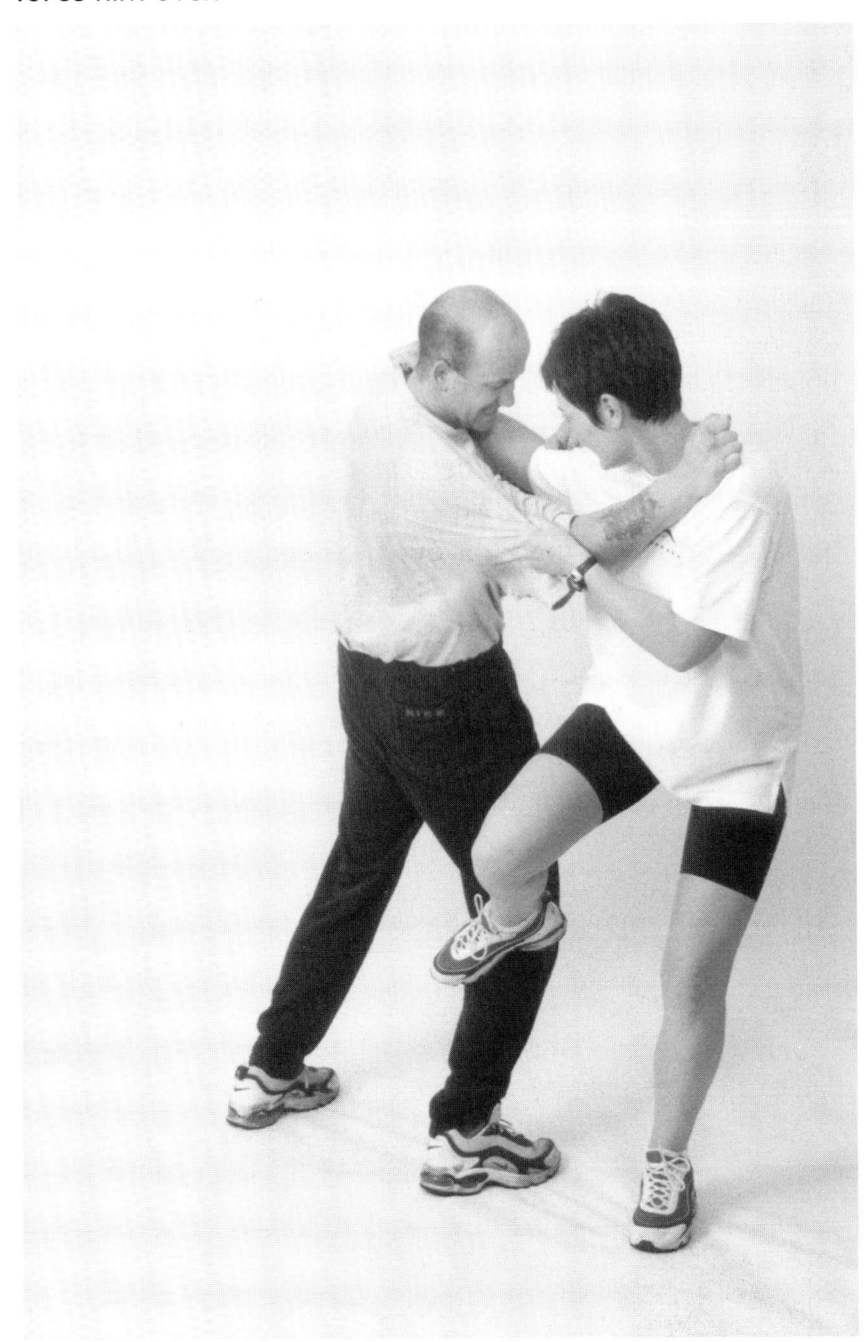

Chapter Eleven

Sweeping kicks

Whilst outside of grappling range I class 'sweeps' as kicks, whilst inside grappling range I class them as sweeps/take downs/ throws. Because this is a book on kicking and not grappling (though I do have a book on grappling if, at all, you are interested) I will keep it to those that do not need the appendage of a grappling adversary.

Used to sweep an opponent's legs from under him. Devastating if followed by a stamping kick. May be used to attack the opponent's front leg, inside or out and rear leg, inside or out. When attacking the front leg the object is to sweep a single leg and force the opponent over, if attacking the rear leg the object is to take both legs at once, literally kicking the opponent's legs from under him. Either should leave the opponent at worst (for him) off balance and vulnerable to a greater attack, at best (for you) completely toppled.

FRONT LEG SWEEP

Used to attack an opponent's leading leg (right or left). Attack the outside shin of the opponent's lead leg with the instep of your attacking foot, sweeping his leg across the front of his own body spiralling him to the floor. This is especially effective if you catch the leg as weight is being transferred onto it, i.e. if the opponent has just replaced it to the floor after an attack (usually a kick) or if he is moving forward.

You can attack with your lead leg or reverse leg and to the inside of the opponent's ankle or the outside, depending up whether he is south paw or orthodox. If you sweep the inside (see illus.) of the opponent's ankle he usually falls forward, if you attack the outside of the ankle he usually falls back.

It is also possible to sweep the opponent's back leg (as a single leg and not a double leg sweep) with either your lead leg or back leg, though to do so takes a lot of skill because you have to travel across the front of the opponent, still using the instep against the inside of the opponent's ankle, to attack.

HOOK SWEEP

Alternatively you can execute the same sweeps employing a hook on contact as opposed to a sweep. For instance, in the case of the front leg sweep, on contact with the opponent's ankle hook your instep around the ankle and pull the leg back towards yourself, forcing the opponent over.

BACK LEG SWEEP

This is a highly skilled technique involving 100% commitment. I utilised it on the pavement arena (I have a book by the same name, you know) many times, often scoring K.O. with it. It relies heavily up on the opponent who is standing with his feet close together (or on a sparring partner who is in the habit of pivoting on one leg). Attack with your strongest side, again using the instep of the foot and attacking the back of the opponent's knees, lifting him completely off the ground, toppling him to the floor. With full commitment it is possible to K.O. the opponent with the back leg sweep/kick because he whips right over and lands on the back of his head. I find it useful to rush into the opponent when applying the back leg sweep, this closes the gap, adds momentum to the attack and often forces the opponent onto his toes (sometimes even one leg) deeming him more vulnerable to the attack.

The same technique may also be employed to the front of the opponent's legs, sweeping/kicking him forward and onto his face. The technique is a facsimile to the back leg sweep hitting the ankles just below the knees as opposed to the back of the knees. When attacking in this way there is the danger of bashing your own shins in execution.

Chapter Twelve

Spinning and crescent kicks

I find spinning kicks, for the live scenario, about as useful as a castor sugar jet ski. Again this is not to say that spinning kicks do not or cannot work, it is just that the skill factor and danger factors are too high and the empirical success rate far to low. As I have already mentioned the success of this kick is largely determined by the elements, by forces that we have little control over and contributing factors like ground surface being wet or uneven, even icy, and the fact that very few attackers will stand off and give you the kind of distance that you need to spin and kick (though I admit they did work very well in Enter The Dragon). In perfect conditions (what are they?) spinkicks can be devastating. These kind of conditions, though, are very rarely found in the 'live' scenario, and you could do as much damage with a punch that moves only six inches and risks nothing.

I spent ten years perfecting my kicking technique, spending much of that time working on the spins. As soon as I started working the doors I stopped practising flashy kicks, like the spinning kick. Even in the 'square go' I wouldn't want to risk 'spinning', if you fall you've lost. Probably the only kick I would consider would be the spinning straight back kick, which has the lowest skill factor of all the spinning kicks but still takes a highly skilled kicker to utilise in a real fight.

The crescent kick is another 'movie kick' that is probably less useful (in a real fight) than a chocolate tea pot. You can spend hours and hours perfecting these kicks in the dojo, but those hours would be wasted. Far better to use the time on the more fundamental and practical front, round and side kicks (all low of course). These kind of kicks look great in demonstrations, they may even work in the controlled arena, in the street? Too risky.

Chapter Thirteen

Drawing

To be perfectly honest 'drawing' is not really a street concept, though at a high level it could be, i.e. in the 'square go' on the common etc. I have used drawing techniques in real fights myself. For this reason and for general interest I have included it in this text. In days of old (when men were bold . . . sorry that's a different book) Samurai would practise 'drawing' an opponent in 'man to man' combat and in 'army to army' warfare, a particular favourite would be for a Samurai to slip and fall to one knee in the midst of a sword fight thus drawing the opponent, believing the fall to be an error, in for the kill. The felled Samurai would then thrust his sword upward and into his opponent as he was about to deliver the coup de grace.

To draw is to tempt or coerce an opponent into a trap by means of tactical play. A little like chess where you lead your opponent to believe that you have made a mistake by deliberately sacrificing a pawn, he takes advantage of the 'supposed' error by 'taking' your offering not realising that in doing so he has left one of his major players unprotected. This may be achieved in one of several ways:

1) By showing the opponent a gap in your defence by dropping or lifting your guard thus exposing the target that you wish to offer as 'bait'. When the opponent attempts to attack the 'bait' you attack him en route.

2) Feign tiredness or injury, tempting your opponent to come in for the kill, when he does 'whack' him.

3) Pretend to retreat so that your opponent may follow, when he does he will walk right on to your kick/attack.

4) Tempt the opponent to sweep your lead leg by pushing it close to him, when he attempts to sweep lift the leg and kick him with it.

5) Throw a weak technique (or several) to convince your opponent that you hold no power so that he feels safe to come in, again to finish you. When he does hit him with a barrage of heavy artillery. One method that I employ is to throw a weak lead leg round house to encourage the opponent to come forward with a counter attack, when he does I kick him with a sharp and penetrative side kick using the same leg.

Of course drawing techniques are many and varied and are often determined by the calibre and genre of fighter in front of you. If he is a forward moving offensive fighter, weak drawing kicks would effectively draw him in to 'bigger' techniques. If he is a retreating , defensive fighter offer him an opening in your defence or feign tiredness/injury/retreat to encourage him to be 'offensive'. The ideal way to practice these techniques is in sparring where experimentation with the different methods will show you what may or may not work. Every fighter is different, what may work on one may not on another. The only way to 'feel' is to practice.

I have had a few situations where I have used feint kicks to make openings for my hands, even fights where I have fought using only feet against boxers because that is their weakest distance and they do not have an understanding of it.

Chapter Fourteen

Feints

Again, whilst this is not specifically an area much used in the street fight and more of a sparring concept it is still worthy of mention. In the 'one on one' fight on the pavement or the common it can, for the advanced, work very well. The feint is akin to 'drawing' in that both are tactical ploys to manufacture 'openings' in an opponent's defence. Whilst the latter does so by encouraging the opponent to attack an opening that isn't really there and then manipulating the opening left by the opponent's irrationality, feinting creates openings in the opponent's defence by pretending to attack one area of the opponent's body, thus drawing his guard to the said attack and then throwing a real attack to the gap left by the falsely deployed guard.

This can be done by feigning a low blow (kick or punch) to draw the opponent's guard down, long enough for you to fill the 'high' gap left, or feigning a high blow to bring the opponent's guard up long enough to attack the 'low' opening. The feint blow and the intended could be any of a myriad as long as they flow and the intended blow fits the opening left by your feint. It is possible, probable and recommended to combine hands and feet when using feints, though not imperative. Potentially, the intended blow can be a 'stopping' strike because the feint has left the intended target area completely unguarded, also because the opponent's mind believes the feint to be an actual attack it doesn't see the intended strike, it is the strike that you don't see that causes the most damage.

As foregoingly described high feints leave low openings and low feints leave high openings, because I feel it impractical to kick high I find it necessary to include the hands in this chapter to act as 'feints'. I see little point in manufacturing high openings for a kick that is impractical. The process will also involve some of the formerly described footwork in Chapter Four, for greater detail on the footwork herein please refer to the relevant chapter. There are many more than the forecoming, mix and match is the order of the day, make your own up, if they work for you then use them.

HALF STEP, KNEE LIFT, LEFT JAB

From a left leading stance (right if reversed) half step forward and lift your left knee as though about to throw a low kick, when the opponent's guard comes away from his face to block the supposed kick jab him in the face.

HALF STEP, KNEE LIFT, BACK LEG SWEEP

From a left leading stance half step forward and lift your left knee as though about to throw a kick, as the opponent reacts to the supposed low kick quickly replace the said foot back on the floor and kick both legs from underneath him with a back leg sweep.

FEINT HIGH JAB, HALF STEP, LOW LEFT ROUND HOUSE (lead leg)

From a left lead stance half step forward with your right leg, at the same time throw a feint jab to the opponent's face, as he lifts his guard to block kick him low with the round house.

You may use any of the basic kicks with this feint, front kick, side kick etc.

FEINT HIGH RIGHT CROSS, BACK LEG ROUND HOUSE

From a left lead stance throw a high right cross to the opponent's face, as he deploys his guard to block, slam a heavy right leg round house in to his unguarded lower lying regions. You may also replace the round house with a front kick.

FEINT ROUND HOUSE, FRONT LUNGE KICK

This technique may be used off the lead leg or the reverse leg. From a left lead stance lift your right knee up and to your right side as though throwing a low round house, as the opponent's guard is deployed to block the round house change it to a front lunge kick, aiming at the opening left.

FEINT LEAD LEG ROUND HOUSE, FRONT LEG SWEEP

From a left lead stance, facing an opponent that is leading with his right leg, lift the knee of your lead left leg as though about to kick round house, as soon as the opponent reacts to the supposed kick quickly replace it back to ground and sweep his right lead leg at the inside ankle, with your right reverse leg.

The list can go on and on. It is important to experiment and find as many as you can, then try to practice and perfect one or two, make them yours.

Chapter Fifteen

Tackling the puncher

A good puncher who understands the mechanics of kicking will be a very hard man to beat, he will simply gobble up kicking distance and stop the kicker operating. However, most good punchers, certainly from my experience, do not understand how a kicker ticks, many in fact feel intimidated by the kicker. It is said that the puncher will always beat the kicker: on the whole I do believe that this is true but there are contributing factors. This statement is working on the premise that the kicker cannot punch and will automatically lose if entering punching range, whilst this is probably true of many kickers it is not true of all. As an over view I would suggest that the all round fighter should be competent in all areas of combat if he/she wishes to survive the urban jungle.

A good puncher is a very dangerous fighter. Once in his own range he will quickly find the K.O. especially against fighters who find the distance foreign. I could tell you how to block jabs, hooks and uppercuts etc. but that is going in to the realms of pugilism, which is out of the context of the book (please refer to Real Punching). Better to keep the puncher in a range that he finds foreign, kicking range (or grappling range if you know it). This is not an easy feat and requires sharp penetrative low kicks that will eventually erode his will. This will be difficult if space is at a premium, which it usually is, though this can be as much to his disadvantage as the kickers because it will probably end in a clinch, then it will be the one who can grapple that will victor.

If I were fighting a puncher, again working on the premise that I don't want to enter punching range (for whatever reason) these are the kind of tactics I would employ.

For greater detail on the prescribed kicks in this and the next two chapters please refer to the relevant chapters describing the said kicks.

ANKLE STOMP

Every time the puncher tries to enter punching range use the ankle stomp to stop him in his tracks. As soon as the kick has landed move, backwards or laterally, out of his range.

GROIN/KNEE KICK

Sharply kick the puncher in the groin or knee, try to do as much damage as possible, kick and move.

FRONT LEG SWEEPS

The puncher will keep pushing forward to acquire his range, as he moves forward and thus transfers weight onto his lead leg sweep it from the inside or out, if he only stumbles you can follow up with a second kick, if he falls, finish him with a stamp.

RUSH AND BACK LEG SWEEP

Again, as the puncher nears rush forward and sweep both legs from the front or the back, when he falls finish with the stamp.

PUBIC BONE SIDE KICK/FRONT KICK/ROUND HOUSE.

Due to the fact that below the belt attacks in boxing are illegal moves, the puncher tends to leave his lower regions unguarded giving the kicker a free shot. As he moves forward kick with all your might at the pubic bone with any of the prescribes kicks.

Again, even if you hurt him he'll probably be looking to counter attack so kick and move.

RETREAT AND BACK KICK

This is an advanced technique that would need much practice and skill to become operational. Working again on the premise that your opponent is moving forward and is undefended to his groin, take a full step back with your left leg (from a left lead stance) so that your right leg is now leading, this will give the impression that you are retreating. As the opponent moves forward spin and attack back kick to his pubic bone, using the left leg. If you catch him moving in this will be a 'stopping' technique, though the timing needs to be very good.

Again there are more techniques along the same lines that you can experiment with, the feints and draws in the relevant chapter will also work well against the puncher and grappler, though to maximise the feet they really need to be combined with the hands.

Chapter Sixteen

Tackling the grappler

I would not be doing my job if I told you that you had much of a chance here. Against anyone that really wants to grab you, you will be grappling. Distance in the real world is lost very quickly, that is why nine out of ten fights end up on the ground. Just recently on our T.V. screens two world champion professional boxers cane to blows after the weigh-in to their much publicised world title bout. These were two of the world's best punchers, within about three seconds they were grappling around the floor. This is how most fights end up.

Against a good grappler who doesn't understand kicking you may well be able to delay the obvious for a short time whilst he figures out how you operate. Against a good grappler who does understand kicking you will be grappling probably within two to three seconds, even if you combine the hands and feet you are still looking at grappling. This is not to slag off the kicker or the puncher, nor to place the grappler on a pedestal, rather it is just an honest evaluation of how I feel it will be.

Again we are working on the premise that the grappler is a good one and not just someone who just thinks he is good and also we are presuming that the kicker will automatically lose if he ends up grappling. The kicker might be a great grappler and if that's the case the more damage he can do to the grappler before it hits the ground the better position he will be in when it does. I work on the three distances: kicking, punching and grappling, this way I am prepared for most eventualities, I feel comfortable in all regions. If you do find yourself facing a grappler it is inevitable that you'll end up in a grappling embrace so the best bet is to try and do as much damage to your adversary as possible, on his way in.

It is important to remember that the grappler (and the puncher) is used to pain. Theirs is a very tactile art, and they will be more than willing to 'take a few' to get in, happy in the belief that they will 'win when in'. Make every attack a damaging one, no half measures, you must try to break the opponent in half with your kick, to do this you must work on power kicking and fast retraction.

There is always the outside chance that you may K.O. him on his way in, if so then the following will not apply.

It is important when dealing with the grappler to kick and move very quickly because he will try to counter your attack by grabbing you into his range. Once you are there it is very difficult to get back out again.

Where techniques are repeated from the last chapter please refer back for more detail.

FINGER KICKING

The grappler relies heavily on the appendage of his fingers, if you can break a couple en route this will help you and hinder him greatly. This is best achieved with sharp front snap kicks (if you'll forgive the pun) aimed at the opponent's finger tips.

ANKLE STOMP

As formerly described, stomp the opponent's ankle as he moves forward and move away quickly.

GROIN/KNEE KICK

Attack the opponent's knees or groin with powerful kicks as he moves forward. Kick and move.

FRONT LEG SWEEP

Attack the opponent's front leg and sweep him to the floor.

RUSH AND BACK LEG SWEEP

This can be effective for the advanced player but beware, in attempting the attack you risk the chance of being grabbed en route and pulled into grappling range.

PUBIC BONE SIDE KICK/FRONT KICK/ROUND HOUSE

As with the pugilist these areas are usually outside the periphery of the grappler's rule book deeming them vulnerable attacking areas, attack hard and fast causing as much damage as possible. Hit and move.

RETREAT AND BACK KICK

Restricted to the skilled practitioner though very effective if successfully employed. Again with this technique you tend to end up rather too close to the opponent so fast retraction and exit is imperative.

Though it is out of the context of this book I would recommend that the reader acquire at least a basic knowledge of boxing and grappling, just in case (or read my books *Real Grappling* & *Real Punching*).

Chapter Seventeen

Tackling the street fighter

It can be pretty difficult to employ kicking technique against the street fighter because he tends to work 'in close' and through dialogue, that is he'll use dialogue to sucker the unsuspecting opponent. He is also heavily into deception so may well act submissive in order to disarm his intended victim. A good street technician with a mastery of 'street speak' will take most people out of the game before they even realise that they are in it.

In the ring the boxer leads with the jab, we all know this so we learn to parry the jab so as to avoid the 'big right', on the pavement the street fighter leads with dialogue but because most people are unaware of this they do not parry the dialogue with counter dialogue and so get stung, usually waking up in a hospital bed wondering 'what the f... went wrong?' What people wrongly assume is that the street fight is some thing akin to a full contact sparring match. This couldn't be further from the truth, the physical fraction of the street encounter rarely lasts longer than a few seconds. If you're dealing with someone that knows the arena well, less than one second. When it does become physical it will be very close range, maybe 18 inches, where kicking is not viable. Of course there are other scenarios where kicking range will be available, but even then only for a fleeting second.

The most effective range available against the street fighter is the hands, the reason for this being the aforementioned 18 inches available to you, but even that will be lost if you do not lock into dialogue and become imminently pre-emptive. From my experience street encounters that go further that the first few seconds end on the ground where the grappler is potentate.

If you do have the distance I can only reiterate the attacks of the last chapter and the recommendation that you:

1) Learn 'street speak' (detailed in Real Self Defence),

2) Obtain a working knowledge of punching and grappling,

3) Learn to combine the three.

FINGER KICKING
As detailed in the last chapters, try to kick and break the opponent's fingers.

ANKLE STOMP
Used as a stop hit to damage the forward moving opponent.

GROIN/KNEE KICKS
While the distance is favourable use sharp, destroying kicks to the opponent's groin/knees/thighs.

FRONT LEG SWEEP
High skill factors involved with this technique but a good 'stopper' if successful.

RUSH AND BACK LEG SWEEP
Same applies here, if you work it you've likely won the fight.

PUBIC BONE SIDE KICK/ROUND HOUSE
Attacking the pubic bone with destroying side kicks (try and hit with the heel) and round house (try and hit with the ball).

RETREAT AND BACK KICK

Draw the opponent on by stepping back, hammer home a low back kick. High skill factor, devastating if effective.

In conclusion, the street fighter lacks very little when it comes to fighting on the pavement. He will and can kick, punch, grapple, bite, butt, scratch and gouge like he was born to do it, he is entering the arena with many ranges in his bag of artillery, all honed in the 'real world' and not in a hypothesised dojo, he knows what he has got works. Because of this array of skills he can and will assess a fighter almost instantly and then fight him/her at their weakest range, forcing the kicker to punch or grapple, the puncher to grapple or kick and the grappler to kick or punch, that is if he hasn't already finished it with the first attack. He will break all the rules, use anything incidental as an appendaged weapon, use deception as his main ally and think nothing of employing the help of a second or third or fourth party to help if you give too much of a fight. To beat these people you have to be these people, you have to be as bad as them to neutralise and worse than them to win, and whilst this might seem a little distasteful so is a severed nose and a hospital bed, which is the alternative.

'If you want to go in to the woods to hunt the Tiger you must first learn everything about the Tiger, his eating habits, the layout of his fighting territory, his sleeping habits, his strengths and his weaknesses, everything. If you do not learn these things you are not hunting the Tiger, you are just going for a walk in the woods.'

Chapter Eighteen

Travelling and centre line extension

Travelling is an advanced concept, though when in the hunt for advancement it is just the natural progression to more power. To travel with a kick (and this doesn't mean taking it on a coach trip to Clacton) is to add the momentum of forward/lateral movement. With punching technique it is far simpler and less risky because the two feet always remain on the floor, with the kick the danger level heightens because invariably you are on the one foot and it doesn't take an intelligent man to realise that this can impair the balance. It can work with any of the kicks though the skill factor of the travel rises with the skill factor of the kick.

There are two forms of travel, the step and the shuffle (sounds like 'come dancing'). The half step, double step, backward step etc. are all detailed in Chapter Four, Footwork (please refer back for greater detail), and all add momentum to a given kick. The shuffle (this can even be a small jump) is, as the name implies, a shuffle or forward thrust at the end of the kick that can add devastating momentum as well as helping to gain distance. Whilst the shuffle may seem easy its practice is hard, kicking technique must first be perfected before engagement in travelling and centre line extension.

FRONT KICKS

At the end of the kick, as it connects with target shuffle/thrust, forward on the support leg. The shuffle may be short or long according to how much travel you want to add or distance you have to cover.

SIDE KICKS

At the end of the kick shuffle/thrust forward on the support leg.

BACK KICK

At the end of the kick, shuffle/thrust forward on the support foot. With the back kick this is a little more advanced due to the 'spin' involved. Much practice would be necessary to perfect.

CENTRE LINE EXTENSION

(This technique is only really viable when employing lateral (as opposed to straight) techniques like the round house kicks, back spinning kick, back roundhouses etc.)

Centre line extension can apply to both punching and kicking (though it is limited to the aforementioned kicks) involving the lateral extension of your own centre line to give your punch more power potential.

The centre line is in line with your opponent's, this allows you only a few inches of extension through the opponent with your kick or punch.

Extend your centre line and thus your punch/kick potential by simply stepping with your left leg to your own left (or right if employing a left side technique). The greater the step the bigger the extension of centre line and thus the more power potential you get. The momentum of the step also adds 'travel' to the extension.

LEFT ROUND HOUSE (lead leg) WITH CENTRE LINE EXTENSION

From a left lead stance lift the knee of your left leg up and to your left side, throw the designated leg around and into the target by pivoting on the support foot and thrusting the hips behind the technique and on impact with the target, as the attacking foot is about to connect with target shuffle across to your own right, on the support foot, to extend centre line. After contact recover the kicking foot quickly to the ground by pulling the hips back to their original position.

RIGHT ROUND HOUSE (back leg) WITH CENTRE LINE EXTENSION

From a left lead stance lift the knee of your right, rear leg up and to your own right side, throw the designated leg around and into the target by pivoting on the support foot and thrusting the hips behind the kick and on impact with the target, as the attacking foot is about to connect with target shuffle across on the support foot to your own left to extend centre line. After connection with target recover the leg quickly by retracting the hip and placing the kicking foot on the ground to your front or bringing it back to its original starting place at the rear.

Centre line extension and 'travel' are both advanced concepts, I would therefore advise the novice kicker to perfect the basic technique of kicking with body weight transference before attempting this advancement.

Chapter Nineteen

The angular graph of kicking

The martial arts seem to be unique in their conventionality, most certainly with the more traditional systems: a side kick is a side kick and a front kick is a front kick, any diversification of tradition is not recognised. If the attacking foot isn't positioned 'just so' and the support leg is incorrectly stationed then the technique is wrong, even if it is effective. This isn't unique to the martial field, a lot of dye hard boxers also insist that their way is the only way and 'change' is sacrilege. This head in the sand attitude of course comes from wearing blinkers for too long.

Real martial art should develop 'enlightenment', (a quality many supposed martial artists claim to have) which in layman's terms is 'the blinkers off'. With the new found 360 degree peripheral vision (and awareness) one is able to see that no one system holds all the answers, no one kick is right or wrong, no one way is the only way. Everything has its good and bad, different systems are not like oil and water in that they will not or cannot mix. If you want to kick side kick and use the ball of the foot as the attacking tool then why not, if you want to throw a kick that is half front and half round then, as long as it does the job and causes you no injury in the process then go ahead. As martial artists we are always being told that our way is the only way and that bastardised techniques are 'bad form', told to keep our movements uniformed otherwise they won't work and we certainly will not pass a grading.

Obviously there is an optimum way of doing a given technique but what is my optimum way may not be yours, 'one man's meat is another man's poison' as they say. It is also true that one should have a base, learning a given technique or a set of movements in the style of our choosing, you need to learn the full route before you can start taking short cuts. The most powerful kick is probably the one that uses full hip and hara, this doesn't mean that a kick that isn't using full hip and hara isn't going to be strong. Some of the deviations forecoming may not be as strong as the full, unchanged kick but they will still 'do the damage'.

Once you have a base kick you need to be working on the different angles the kick can be thrown at and whether, at the right range it might mix well with another, like for instance the thigh kick, it is neither a round house nor is it a front kick, it is a cross between the two. One thing is for sure, no one can deny the power of the kick even if it is not aesthetically endowed. This is where the angular graph of kicking comes in, it is a way of tailoring kicking technique to any given target or opening enabling you to mix and match different kicks to fit a small gap in the opponent's armoury where perhaps one of the base kicks would have found no entry (some of you will have probably been doing this anyway with out realising it - understanding the process can help you to manipulate it)

To explain this in greater detail I shall use three graphs, 1) for front and round house kicks, 2) for front and side kicks 3) for side and straight back kicks.

The graph system also works with the more superfluous spinning kick though I have not excluded them herein because of the nature of the text.

The graphs for angular kicking work almost in a facsimile for my 'graph of angular punches' in the book Real Punching so please forgive me if I am going over familiar ground (familiar to those who have read the punching book).

1) FRONT AND ROUND HOUSE KICK

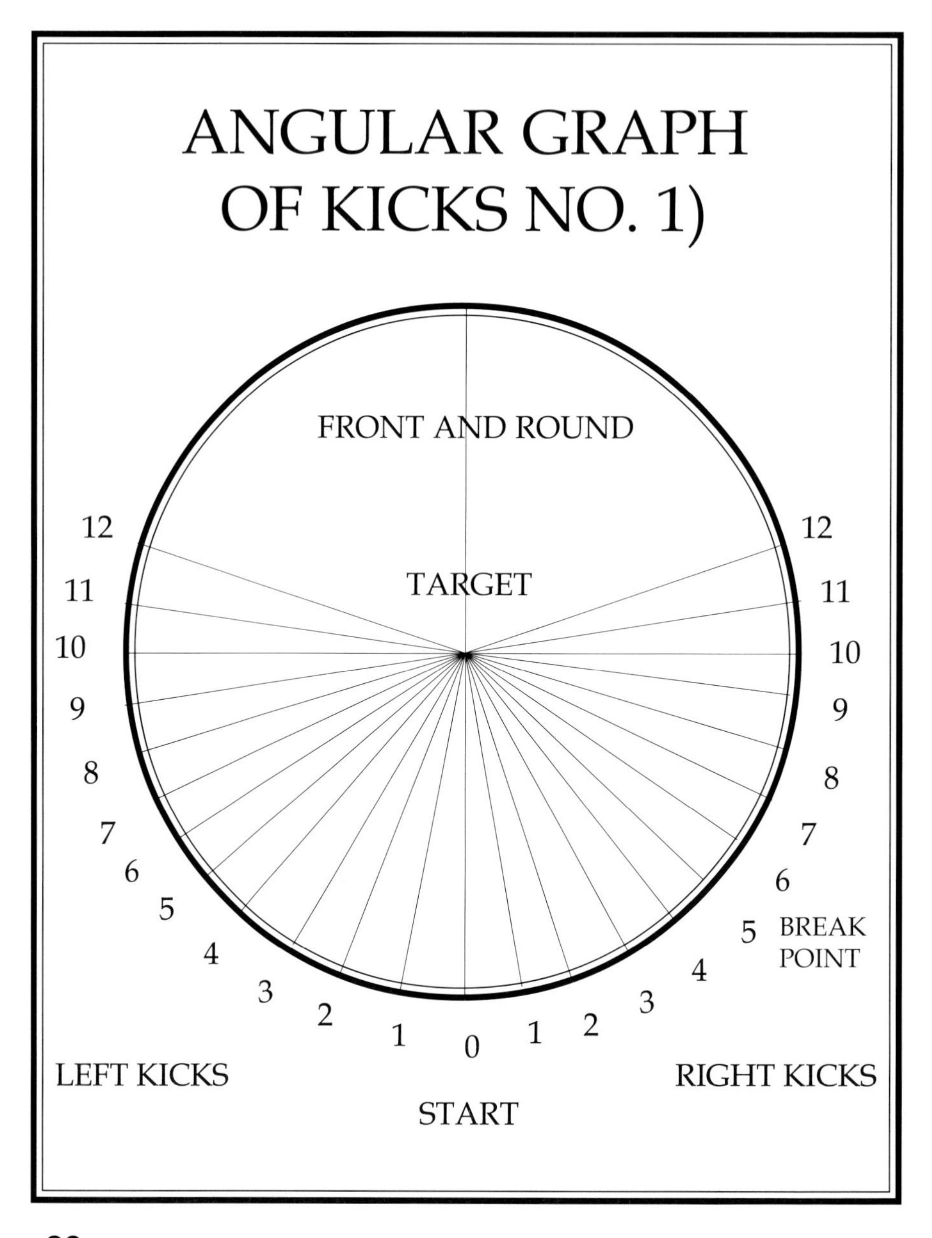

Kicker is standing on start position, facing target on the graph.

0-TARGET on the graph represents the straight front kick, left or right.

10 represents the conventional round house kick, left or right.

11 & 12 represent the over hand round house kick, left or right.

All the numbers in between, from 1-9, represent angled variations of the two conventionals.

The left side of the graph represents left kick variations, the right side of the graph, right kick variations.

In the case, for instance, of the basic right leg front kick, it starts out in a straight line that travels between 0 & Target. If the route to target is obstructed the kicker may chose to throw the kick along angle No.1, adding a slight turn to the kick, or angle 2, 3 or 4 if a greater angle is required. All of these kicks would be classed as 'hooked' front kicks, the hook becomes more prominent the higher the angle number you chose.

No. 5 on the graph is the 'break point', this is where the technique becomes more of a round house that a front kick and therefore becomes classed as a 'straight round house'. As the angle becomes more acute, 6,7 and 8 etc. the kick becomes more and more hooked until at angle 10 it becomes the conventional round house. This process of course can be reversed if you start at angle 10, the conventional round house and work your way down the scale, back through the break point where the kick becomes more straight than hooked and eventually back to '0' where we again have the straight, conventional front kick.

Angles 11 & 12 are for those of us who are supple and can get knee lift high enough to bring the kick above the target area and then back down.

2) FRONT AND SIDE KICKS

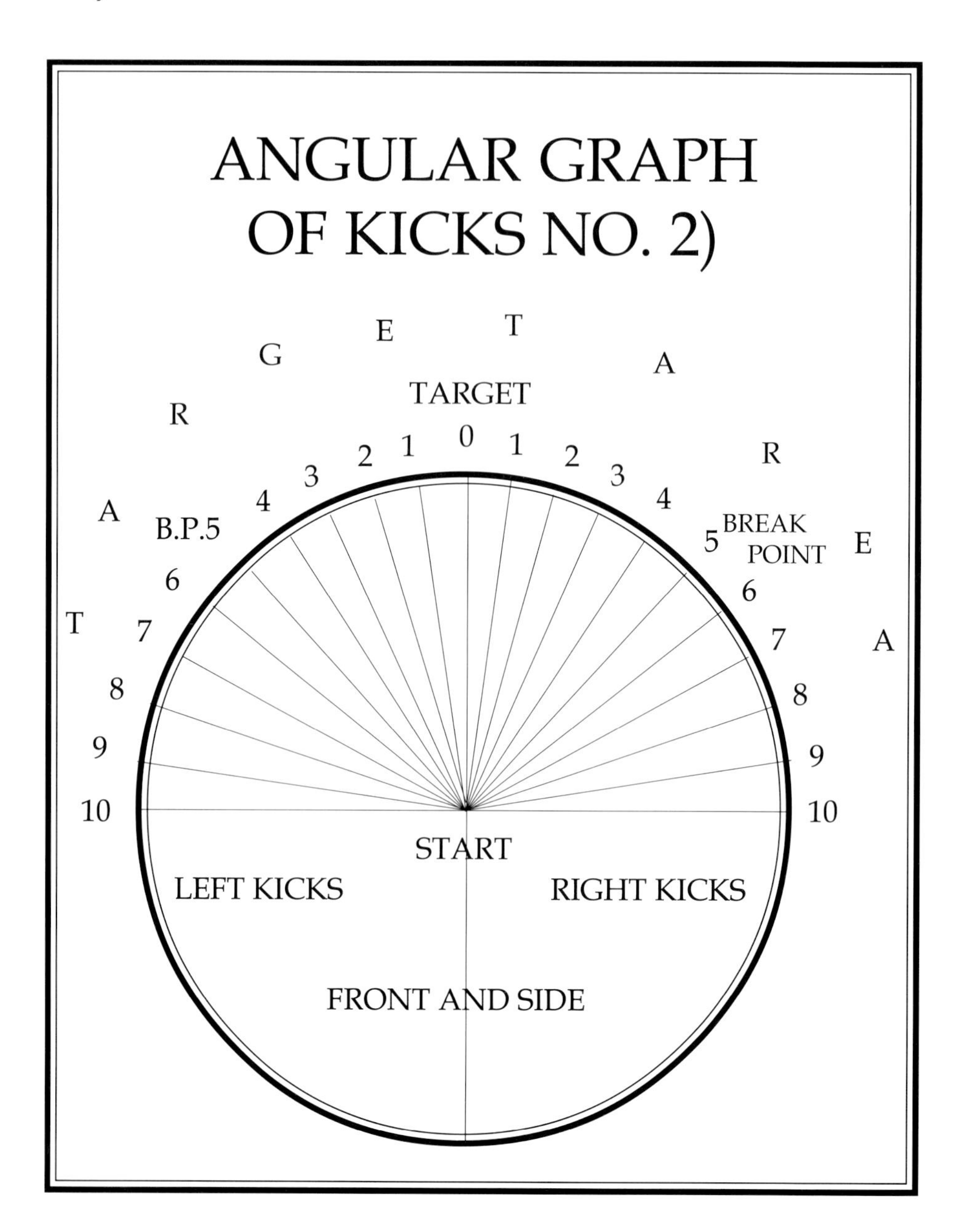

As you'll have noticed (you perceptive devil you) graph 2) is inverted with the target areas being on the outside of the graph as opposed to the inside centre on graph 1). Graph 1) deals with making angles to fit openings, graphs 2) and 3) deal with the opponent or multiple opponents who approach from different angles and the kicker affecting kicking technique to meet those angles. We are working on the premise that the attack needs to be very quick and/or you may be grappling (vertically) with another opponent so you are not able to change centre line (face the opponent) and throw a conventional front or side kick, though if that option is open to you, you may wish to employ conventionality. The graph works on the fact that you do not have to change centre line to attack effectively, if you do change centre line the kicks are not longer 'angular'.

Kicker is standing at start facing directly forward to '0' and target on graph. 'START' - '0' on the graph represents the straight front kick, left or right. START - 10 represents the traditional side kick. All the numbers between, from 1-9, represent angled variations of the two conventionals. The left side of the graph represents left sided kicks, the right side of the graph, right sided kicks.

Starting again with the basic front kick which travels along the line 0 to 0, if the opponent comes at an angle off centre you may choose to throw the kick along angle 1, 2, 3 or 4, depending upon his approach route. Once you reach angle 5, break point, the kick becomes more of a side kick than a front kick and so on right up the angle graph through 6, 7, 8 and 9 until at angle 10 the kick becomes the conventional side kick. And as with graphs 1 & 3 the process may be reversed by starting at angle 10, side kick, and working back to 0, front kick. The angle of the foot when changing angles need not matter, as long as it is taught and the toes pulled back for protection.

3) SIDE AND BACK KICKS

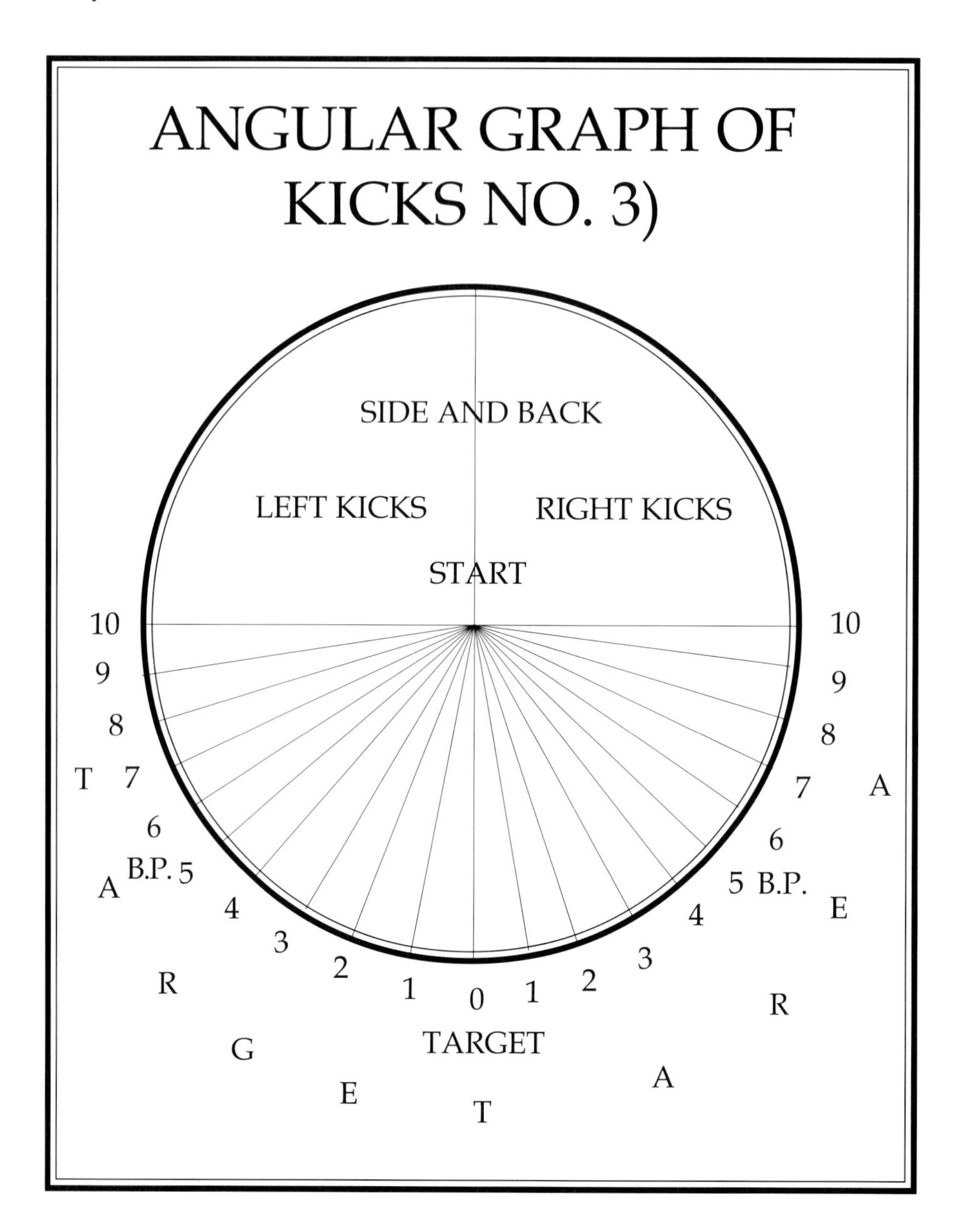

On graph 3) we start where we finished off on graph 2), at angle 10, the basic side kick, and working slowly backwards along the angles until we reach straight back kick.

Kicker is standing at 'start' body to the front but looking sideways to angle 10.

Start to 10 on the graph represents the conventional side kick.

Start to '0' represents the basic straight back kick.

All the numbers in between, from 9-1, represent angled variations of the two conventionals.

The left side of the graph represents left kick variations, the right side of the graph, right variations.

As previously described in graphs 1) and 2) we change the angle of the kick without having to alter centre line, as with graph 2), graph 3) has the angle of the kick varying to meet the approach of an off-centre opponent rather than, as in graph 1), altering the angle of the kick to fill a gap in the opponent's armoury.

Starting with the conventional side kick from 'start' to angle 10 we may, again, change the angle of the kick along numbers 9, 8, 7 and 6, when we reach angle 5 the kick becomes more of a back kick than a side kick. Eventually as we go through angles 4, 3, 2 and 1 the kick becomes more and more straight until at '0' we have the basic, straight back kick. This may also be reversed by starting at '0', basic back kick, and working back the same way, through 1, 2, 3, 4, 5 break point, 6, 7, 8, 9, and eventually 10, the conventional side kick.

Using the angle theory nearly every kick you throw will be different from the last, each one varying in angle. This, in theory, will give you an infinite number of kicks to chose from, all born from the conventional front, side, back and round house. If you get a chance take a look at some of the Bruce Lee films and see the different angles he uses for kicking (ignore the fact that they are high kicks, they work the same low) you'll find it very hard to put a name tag on any of the kicks because they are all angled variations of each other.

Chapter Twenty

Training equipment

The very best way to train the feet is to teach them how to run, that way you won't have to use them to kick people. Other than that I would recommend the six foot punch bag for the development low, crushing kicks and sweeps. This training aid will develop timing (if you swing the bag and kick it on its return), power (practising for power will also develop technique because it's pretty hard to get decent power without correct technique), distancing (vary the distance that you stand from the bag so as to work different ranges), travelling & centre line extension (all the prescribed exercises in the relevant chapters can be practised on the bag), and foot work (don't just use the bag to develop power like so many do, treat it with a bit of respect, spar with it, practise like you would with a partner).

The strike shield is also an invaluable implement for developing all of the foregoing, focus pads are perfect for the development of accuracy, a skill so often ignored in today's martial arts, training with the focus pads will develop pin-point accuracy so that when you throw a kick it does its job, nothing's gained when you hit a heavily muscled or boned area of the opponent's anatomy, and of course, last but not least, the 'live' training partner. To pressure test your kicking ability try progressive sparring with your partner, allow kicking, punching, grappling, anything that he wants to do, and encourage him to try and catch your kicks if they are slow, pushy or if you pivot on one leg for to long. This will sharpen up your kicks and footwork immeasurably.

Epilogue

As I have always said, and as I'm sure your aware, a kick is definitely more than just a kick. The kicking arts are as intricate as any other with a lot of hard work needed to find competence.

Good kickers, I have known only a few, will contradict every warning inscribed herein about the limits of effective kicking in a 'live' scenario. That is their prerogative as brilliant kickers, they are 9's and 10's (on a skill scale of one to ten), the cream of the kicking arts. They would probably make everything and anything work, but that doesn't help if you are an 8, 7, 6, 5, 4, 3, 2 or 1 or if the people you are teaching are. An average kicker would not be able to kick his way out of a wet paper bag, an average puncher or grappler now, that's a different kettle of fish. Kicking is a wonderful art and I'm not about to knock that, just let's keep it in context and use them only when they're safely called for. Most people that tell me they think they could effectively introduce kicking into the ugliness of a real fight haven't been there, those that have are usually always very exceptional human beings (or at the least very exceptional kickers).

I worked on the door for a long time with probably the best puncher I have ever witnessed, a professional boxer. His hands were excellent and yet all he wanted was to kick, every night we worked he would have me teaching him to kick (gladly exchanged for boxing lessons). The reason he was so infatuated by kicking was because he'd witnessed the decimation of five men outside a nightclub in London, by a young man who could really kick. Whenever we got in to a situation outside the nightclub my friend would try to employ the kicks he so adored: all it got him was trouble where he had quickly to revert back to hands.

When the circumstances are right and the distance favourable kicking technique can be second to none, I have had several K.O.'s with kicking, but then I've been in or around thousands of fights. Percentage wise I'd say I've used my feet in 5% of all situations, and that was mostly sweeps.

Train your feet to back up your hands, train your grappling to back up your hands & your feet, learn 'street speak' and be pre-emptive and above all be aware and you'll find that those situations that you can't avoid you'll win.